Simple Machines in the Military

Gillian Gosman

PowerKiDS press.

New York

For Roger and George

Published in 2015 by The Rosen Publishing Group, Inc.
29 East 21st Street, New York, NY 10010

First Edition

Book Design: Joe Carney
Photo Research: Katie Stryker

Photo Credits: Cover Rob Byron/Shutterstock.com; pp. 4, 10 Stocktrek Images/Thinkstock; p. 5 Mike Watson Images/moodboard/Thinkstock; p. 6 George Xu/Shutterstock.com; pp. 7, 18 U.S. Navy/Handout/Getty Images; p. 8 Donald Gargano/Shutterstock.com; p. 9 (top) Joseph Devenney/Photographer's Choice/Getty Images; p. 9 (bottom) Africa Studio/Shutterstock.com; p. 11 NorGal/Shutterstock.com; p. 12 Christopher Futcher/E+/Getty Images; p. 13 Dmitro/Shutterstock.com; pp. 14, 15, 17 (top) Stocktrek Images/Getty Images; p. 16 Terry Moore/Stocktrek Images/Getty Images; p. 17 (bottom) Soon Wee hong/Shutterstock.com; p. 19 Buyenlarge/Contributor/Archive Photos/Getty Images; p. 20 Taeya18/Shutterstock.com; p. 21 Nadezhda Bolotina/Shutterstock.com; p. 22 Stocktrek Images/Vetta/Getty Images.

Library of Congress Cataloging-in-Publication Data

Gosman, Gillian, author.
 Simple machines in the military / by Gillian Gosman. – First edition.
     pages cm. – (Simple machines everywhere)
 Includes index.
 ISBN 978-1-4777-6833-4 (library binding) – ISBN 978-1-4777-6834-1 (pbk.) – ISBN 978-1-4777-6641-5 (6-pack)
 1. Simple machines—Juvenile literature. 2. Machinery—Juvenile literature. 3. Vehicles, Military—Juvenile literature. I. Title.
 TJ147.G685 2015
 621.8–dc23
                    2013048289

Manufactured in the United States of America

CPSIA Compliance Information: Batch #WS14PK5: For Further Information contact Rosen Publishing, New York, New York at 1-800-237-9932

Contents

What Are Simple Machines?

Simple machines are tools that help us do work by increasing the amount of **effort**, or force, we apply to a job. The greater the force applied, the more **motion** will result. By using simple machines, we are able to apply more force and get greater motion while using less of our own energy.

An inclined plane helps this amphibious assault vehicle drive off a ship into the ocean. "Amphibious" means that this vehicle can travel by water and by land.

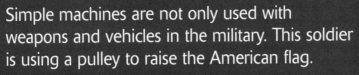

Simple machines are not only used with weapons and vehicles in the military. This soldier is using a pulley to raise the American flag.

The six simple machines are the inclined plane, the wedge, the screw, the lever, the pulley, and the wheel and axle. Simple machines are very important to the military. They have been throughout history and still are today. In this book, you will learn about many of the ways the military uses simple machines.

The Plane Truth

This helicopter has its ramp lowered. Big military helicopters can carry large amounts of cargo. They can also carry trucks and other vehicles. Those vehicles simply drive up the ramp into the helicopter!

An inclined plane is a **surface** with one raised end. Objects can be moved along the surface from one end of the inclined plane to the other. Moving an object along a **slope** requires less effort than lifting or lowering the object the height of the plane.

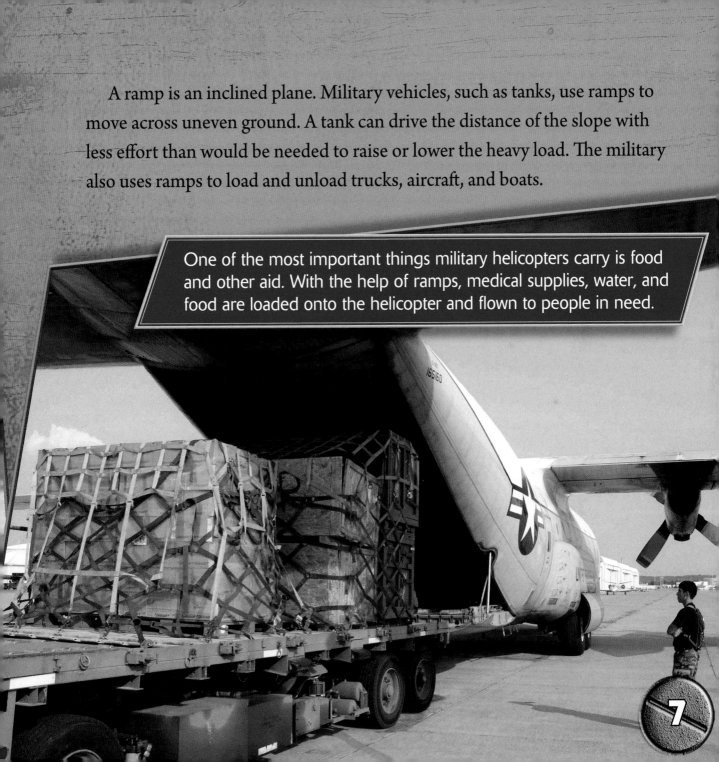

A ramp is an inclined plane. Military vehicles, such as tanks, use ramps to move across uneven ground. A tank can drive the distance of the slope with less effort than would be needed to raise or lower the heavy load. The military also uses ramps to load and unload trucks, aircraft, and boats.

One of the most important things military helicopters carry is food and other aid. With the help of ramps, medical supplies, water, and food are loaded onto the helicopter and flown to people in need.

The Wonders of the Wedge

A wedge does two important jobs. It drives things apart and draws them together. When its **narrow** edge is inserted into an object, the effort we apply to the wedge is multiplied and redirected sideways. A knife is a wedge that drives two pieces apart, while a nail is a wedge that can hold two pieces together.

This is the USS *Joseph P. Kennedy*, a Gearing-class destroyer. This Navy ship was in use from 1945 until 1973. Its wedge-shaped body helped it cut smoothly through the water on its many missions around the world.

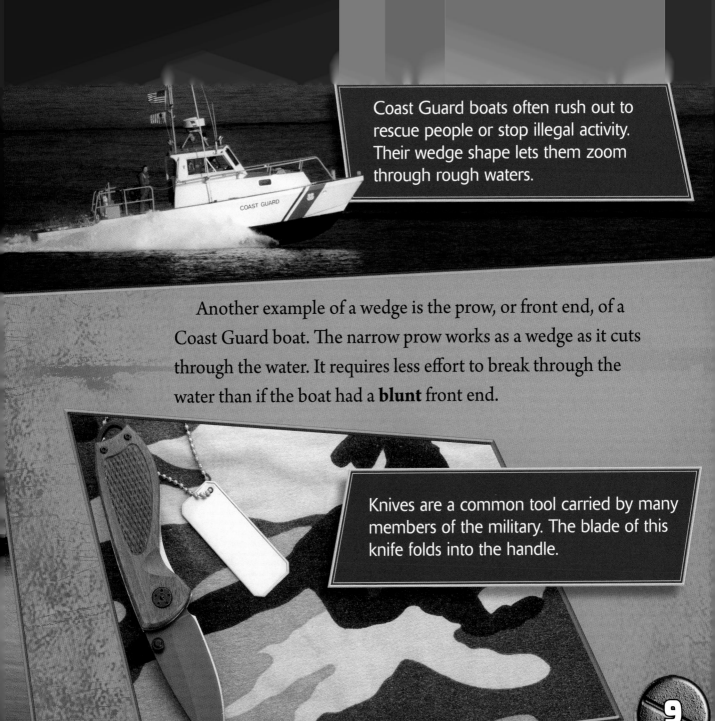

Coast Guard boats often rush out to rescue people or stop illegal activity. Their wedge shape lets them zoom through rough waters.

Another example of a wedge is the prow, or front end, of a Coast Guard boat. The narrow prow works as a wedge as it cuts through the water. It requires less effort to break through the water than if the boat had a **blunt** front end.

Knives are a common tool carried by many members of the military. The blade of this knife folds into the handle.

Super Screws

Here, you can see a rotor in action. These powerful, fast-moving blades lift huge helicopters off the ground, allowing them to carry troops and supplies across the world!

A screw is often thought of as a thin **cylindrical** bar with one flat end and one pointed end. A ridge runs around the shaft, or length, of the bar. This ridge is called the **thread**. When force is applied to the flat end, the screw twists into an object. The thread multiplies the effort, lifting the material around it.

The rotor, or spinning blades, of a helicopter is a screw, too! The engine provides the effort and turns the blades, and the blades move the air around them. This creates the lift that raises the aircraft off of the ground.

Thread

The screw is even found in the simplest of military supplies. This canteen has a thread running around its mouth, which allows the top to be securely screwed on.

Launched by a Lever!

Effort

Fulcrum

Load

Here, you can see a Navy sailor using oars to row a boat. The oars act as levers, pushing the water back and propelling the boat forward.

A lever is a plank that **pivots** on a **fulcrum**, or fixed point. A lever can lift, push, or pull a load. There are three classes of levers. They are grouped by the location of the fulcrum in relation to the load and effort.

An ancient catapult is a lever. Early stone-throwing machines came in many shapes and sizes. For example, the mangonel is a third-class lever. The fulcrum is at one end, the load at the other end, and the effort is stored in the tightened rope holding down the plank in the middle.

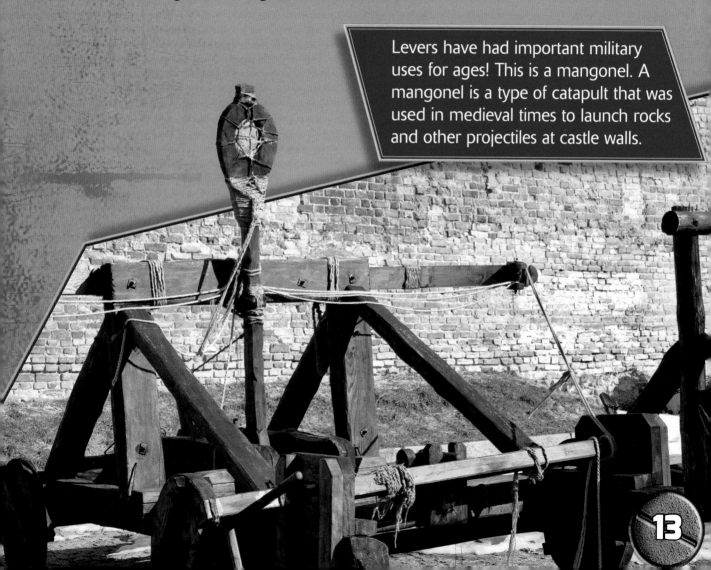

Levers have had important military uses for ages! This is a mangonel. A mangonel is a type of catapult that was used in medieval times to launch rocks and other projectiles at castle walls.

Popular Pulleys

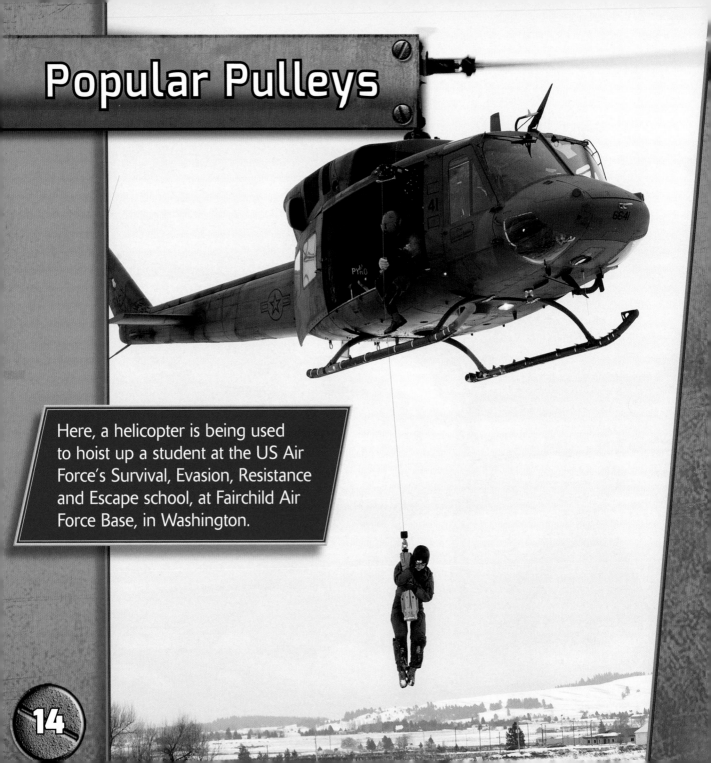

Here, a helicopter is being used to hoist up a student at the US Air Force's Survival, Evasion, Resistance and Escape school, at Fairchild Air Force Base, in Washington.

A pulley is a wheel that turns around a fixed rod. Usually a groove runs along the outer edge of the wheel, and a rope, chain, or cable is set in this groove. Effort is applied to one end of the rope, chain, or cable to raise a load attached to the other end of the line.

Pulleys were very common on the early sailing vessels used by the great navies of history. Made of wood, the pulleys, called blocks, were used to raise and lower the enormous sails and rotate, or turn, the sails to catch the wind.

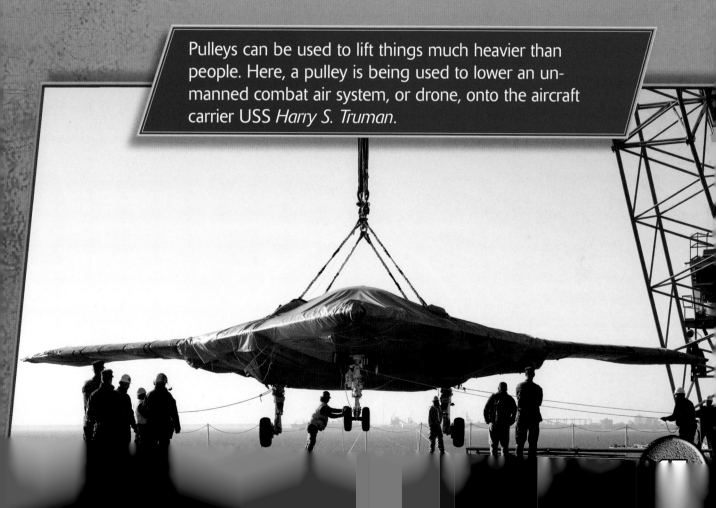

Pulleys can be used to lift things much heavier than people. Here, a pulley is being used to lower an un-manned combat air system, or drone, onto the aircraft carrier USS *Harry S. Truman*.

The Wheel and Axle

A wheel and axle is made up of a large wheel attached to a smaller rod called an axle. Applying effort to rotate the axle also makes the wheel rotate. The wheel's larger **circumference** means that its rotation covers more ground than the axle's rotation alone would. Rotating a wheel makes the attached axle spin, too. This is how a steering wheel works.

The military makes great use of the wheel and axle. Every tank, transport truck, and armored vehicle makes its way thanks to the rotation of wheel and axles.

This is an Oshkosh MRAP, or mine-resistant and ambush-protected, all-terrain vehicle. It has special features to keep the soldiers inside safe.

147-inch wheel circumference

23-inch axle circumference

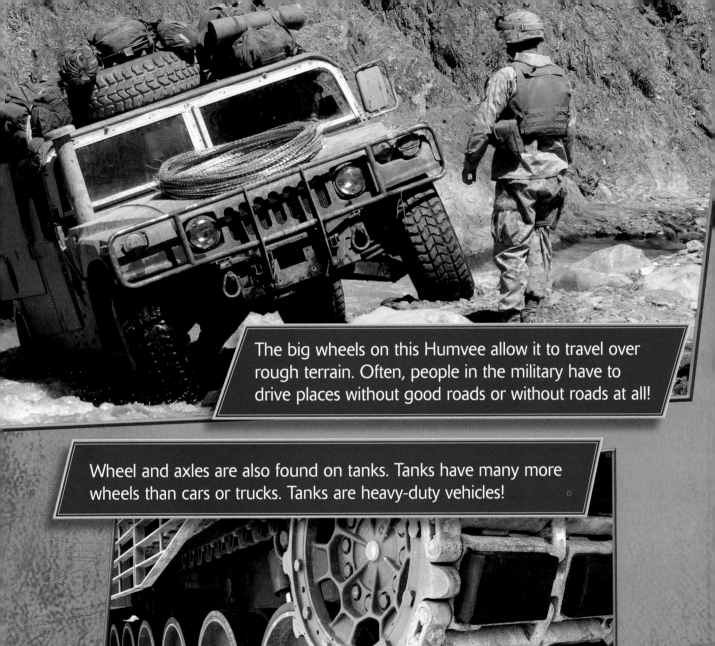

The big wheels on this Humvee allow it to travel over rough terrain. Often, people in the military have to drive places without good roads or without roads at all!

Wheel and axles are also found on tanks. Tanks have many more wheels than cars or trucks. Tanks are heavy-duty vehicles!

Simple Machines in Military History

Members of the military have many jobs other than combat. They are also called in to help out in disasters. Here, members of the Navy are using wheelbarrows to clear out a building damaged by Hurricane Katrina.

The six simple machines we have studied have been around since the earliest human civilizations were building, exploring, and waging war. Many weapons, such as spears, arrows, and swords, are wedges. Catapults and their close cousins crossbows were long used to lob stones and arrows into the castles and walled cities of early civilizations during battles.

While mangonel catapults are third-class levers, wheelbarrows are second-class levers. The wheelbarrow was invented by the Chinese nearly 2,000 years ago to carry medical supplies on the battlefields, according to some accounts.

Simple machines have played an important role in American military history. This US Army armored truck with a machine gun mounted on it is from the 1910s.

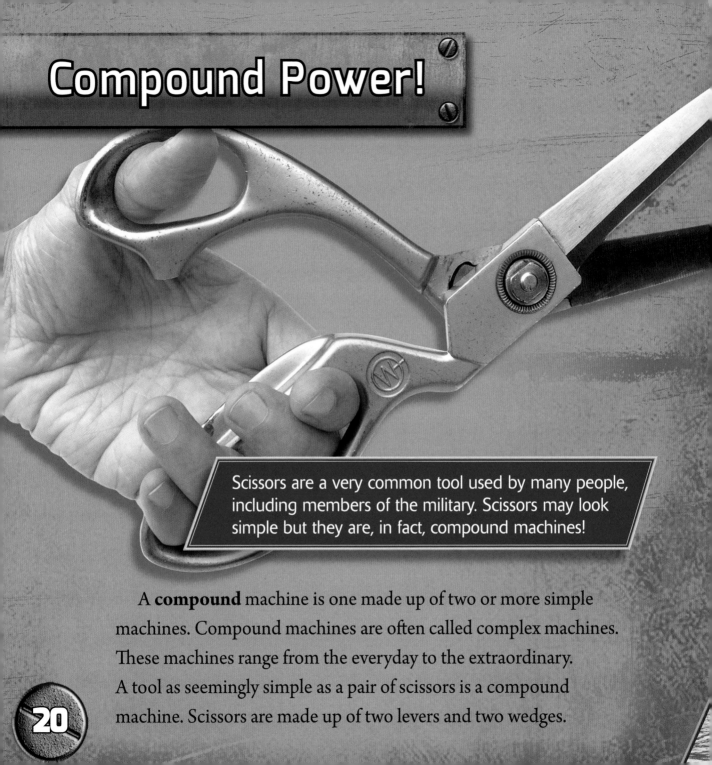

Compound Power!

Scissors are a very common tool used by many people, including members of the military. Scissors may look simple but they are, in fact, compound machines!

A **compound** machine is one made up of two or more simple machines. Compound machines are often called complex machines. These machines range from the everyday to the extraordinary. A tool as seemingly simple as a pair of scissors is a compound machine. Scissors are made up of two levers and two wedges.

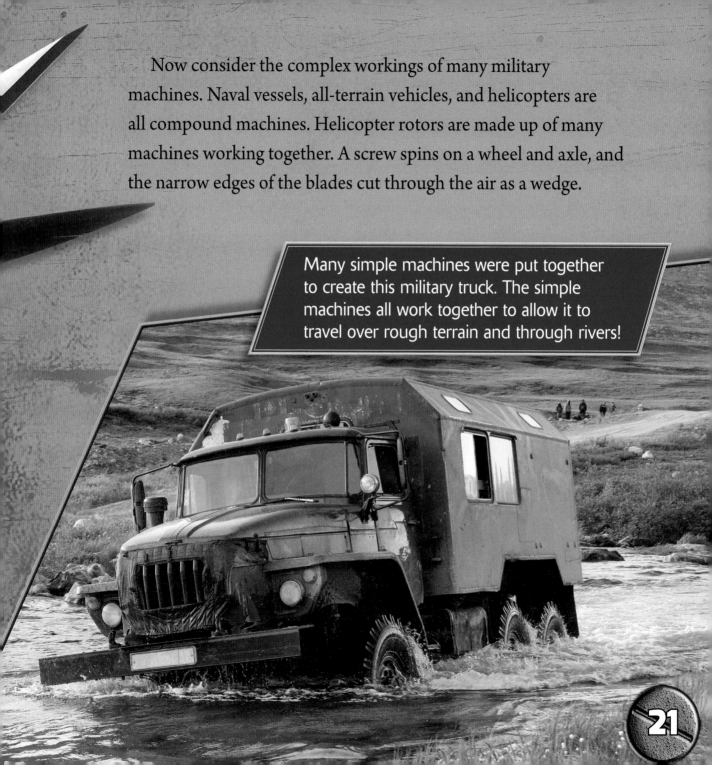

Now consider the complex workings of many military machines. Naval vessels, all-terrain vehicles, and helicopters are all compound machines. Helicopter rotors are made up of many machines working together. A screw spins on a wheel and axle, and the narrow edges of the blades cut through the air as a wedge.

Many simple machines were put together to create this military truck. The simple machines all work together to allow it to travel over rough terrain and through rivers!

The Simple Life

Simple machines are all around us and have been for thousands of years. People have used them to do work since earliest recorded history. Life has gotten more complicated and so have our machines, but simple machines remain central to our daily work. Imagine your life without tools that cut, lift, roll, and hold loads.

The military makes great use of simple machines working both alone and together with other simple machines. They help the military move people and materials. They are parts of weapons and buildings. In short, they are an important part of every military action!

Simple machines and compound machines help the military work. They make up weapons and means of transport. They also help keep people safe!

22

Glossary

blunt (BLUNT) Having a dull edge or point.

circumference (ser-KUMP-fernts) The distance around something circular.

compound (KOM-pownd) Two or more things combined.

cylindrical (suh-LIN-drih-kul) Shaped like a cylinder.

effort (EH-fert) The amount of force applied to an object.

fulcrum (FUL-krum) The point on which a lever pivots.

motion (MOH-shun) Movement.

narrow (NER-oh) Not very wide.

pivots (PIH-vuts) Turns on a fixed point.

slope (SLOHP) A hill.

surface (SER-fes) The outside of anything.

thread (THRED) The raised line that winds around a screw.

Index

C
circumference, 16

E
edge(s), 8, 15, 21
effort, 4, 6–13, 15–16
end, 6, 9–10, 13, 15
energy, 4

F
force, 4, 10

H
height, 6

I
inclined plane, 5–7

L
lever(s), 5, 12–13,
    19–20

M
motion, 4

P
pulley(s), 5, 15

R
ramp(s), 7

S
screw 5, 10–11, 21
slope, 6–7
surface, 6

T
tool(s), 4, 20, 22

W
wedge(s), 5, 8–9,
    18, 20–21
wheel and axle(s), 5,
    16, 21
work, 4, 22

Websites

Due to the changing nature of Internet links, PowerKids Press has developed an online list of websites related to the subject of this book. This site is updated regularly. Please use this link to access the list: www.powerkidslinks.com/sme/mili/

24